C000156056

BABY DON'T SHIT YOUR PANTS

by Cedar White

Illustrated by Vivian Mineker

TO OUR CHILDREN
PLEASE ENJOY THIS BOOK ON THE POTTY

BABY YOU ARE SO BIG
DOING THINGS ON YOUR OWN
BUT WHEN YOU SHIT YOUR PANTS
MOMMY AND DADDY GROAN

WE LOVE YOU AND WE KISS YOU
FEED YOU UNTIL YOU'RE MAD
BABY DON'T SHIT YOUR PANTS
IT MAKES YOUR PARENTS SAD

RELAX NOW ON THE POTTY
DON'T RUSH IT, WE LIKE TO SAY
YOU KNOW I LOVE TO TAKE A SHIT
IT'S THE BEST PART OF MY DAY

JUST SIT A LITTLE LONGER
PLEASE, WAIT A LITTLE MORE

IF YOU GET UP TOO SOON
YOU'LL JUST SHIT ON THE FLOOR

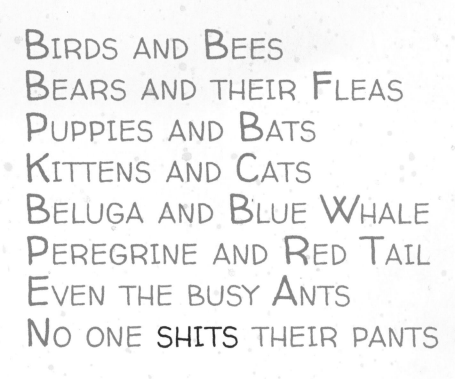

BIRDS AND BEES
BEARS AND THEIR FLEAS
PUPPIES AND BATS
KITTENS AND CATS
BELUGA AND BLUE WHALE
PEREGRINE AND RED TAIL
EVEN THE BUSY ANTS
NO ONE **SHITS** THEIR PANTS

MONKEYS JUMPING
ON THEIR BEDS

WITH SUGAR PLUMS
IN THEIR HEADS

THE TOOTH FAIRY
AND SANTA CLAUS

When you poop in the potty
You'll see your parents dance
But nothing lasts forever
Grandpa just SHIT his pants

THE END
NOW WIPE YOUR ASS, BABY

CEDAR WHITE IS AN AUTHOR LIVING DEEP IN THE OREGON WOODS. HE HAS TWO LITTLE BOYS WHO DEFECATE IN THEIR PANTS, ON THE KITCHEN FLOOR, ON THE CARPET, IN THE BATHTUB, IN THE SINK, IN THEIR SAND-BOX, AND IN THEIR FATHER'S HANDS, AMEN. IN THEIR HOME, A SWEAR JAR IS THE BOYS' COLLEGE-SAVINGS ACCOUNT; THEY COULD GO TO FUCKING HARVARD.

VIVIAN MINEKER IS AN ARTIST AND AN ILLUSTRATOR. FOR HER, EMOTIONALLY CONNECTING WITH OTHERS THROUGH VISUAL STORYTELLING IS HER PASSION. SHE IS AMERICAN, BUT LIVES ABROAD. HER TRAVEL GIVES HER AN OPENNESS THAT SHINES THROUGH IN HER ART. YOU CAN SEE IT RIGHT NOW AT: VIVIANMINEKER.COM OR FOLLOW HER @VIVIAN.MINEKER TO SEE WHAT SHE DOES NEXT.

EXTRA TOILET PAPER
(YOU'RE WELCOME)

CPSIA information can be obtained
at www.ICGtesting.com
Printed in the USA
LVHW071937070721
692098LV00006B/160